Blood Pre

log book

> *Record your reading in this log book and take it to your doctor on your next visit so that she/he can easily diagnose your condition and monitor your progress.*

This book belongs to

Name ------------------------------------

Telephone ------------------------------------

Address ------------------------------------

In case of emergency please contact

Name ------------------------------------

Telephone ------------------------------------

Address ------------------------------------

BLOOD PRESSURE CATEGORIES

BLOOD PRESSURE CATEGORY	SYSTOLIC mm Hg (upper number)	--	DIASTOLIC mm H (lower number)
NORMAL	LESS THAN 120	And	LESS THAN 80
ELEVATE	120-129	and	LESS THAN 80
HIGH BLOOD PRESSURE (HYPERTENSION) STAGE 1	130-139	or	80-89
HIGH BLOOD PRESSURE (HYPERTENSION) STAGE 2	140 OR HIGHER	or	90 OR HIGHER
HYPERTENSIVE CRISIS (consult your doctor immediately)	HIGHER THAN 180	And/or	HIGHER THAN 120

Ways to control high blood pressure

❖ **Lose extra pounds** : *Blood pressure often increases as weight increases.*

❖ **Exercise regularly** : *Regular physical activity — such as 150 minutes a week can lower your blood pressure by about 5 to 8 mm Hg.*

❖ **Eat a healthy diet** : *Eating a diet that is rich in whole grains, fruits, vegetables and low-fat dairy products and skimps on saturated fat and cholesterol.*

❖ **Reduce your stress** : *Chronic stress may contribute to high blood pressure.*

DATE	TIME		SYS/DIA [mmHg]	Heart rate [Pul/min]	NOTES
	am	pm			
	am	pm			
	am	pm			
	am	pm			
	am	pm			
	am	pm			
	am	pm			
	am	pm			
	am	pm			
	am	pm			
	am	pm			
	am	pm			
	am	pm			
	am	pm			
	am	pm			
	am	pm			
	am	pm			

DATE	TIME		SYS/DIA [mmHg]	Heart rate [Pul/min]	NOTES
	am	pm			
	am	pm			
	am	pm			
	am	pm			
	am	pm			
	am	pm			
	am	pm			
	am	pm			
	am	pm			
	am	pm			
	am	pm			
	am	pm			
	am	pm			
	am	pm			
	am	pm			

DATE	TIME		SYS/DIA [mmHg]	Heart rate [Pul/min]	NOTES
	am	pm			
	am	pm			
	am	pm			
	am	pm			
	am	pm			
	am	pm			
	am	pm			
	am	pm			
	am	pm			
	am	pm			
	am	pm			
	am	pm			
	am	pm			
	am	pm			
	am	pm			
	am	pm			
	am	pm			

DATE	TIME		SYS/DIA [mmHg]	Heart rate [Pul/min]	NOTES
	am	pm			
	am	pm			
	am	pm			
	am	pm			
	am	pm			
	am	pm			
	am	pm			
	am	pm			
	am	pm			
	am	pm			
	am	pm			
	am	pm			
	am	pm			
	am	pm			
	am	pm			
	am	pm			

DATE	TIME		SYS/DIA [mmHg]	Heart rate [Pul/min]	NOTES
	am	pm			
	am	pm			
	am	pm			
	am	pm			
	am	pm			
	am	pm			
	am	pm			
	am	pm			
	am	pm			
	am	pm			
	am	pm			
	am	pm			
	am	pm			
	am	pm			
	am	pm			
	am	pm			
	am	pm			
	am	pm			

DATE	TIME		SYS/DIA [mmHg]	Heart rate [Pul/min]	NOTES
	am	pm			
	am	pm			
	am	pm			
	am	pm			
	am	pm			
	am	pm			
	am	pm			
	am	pm			
	am	pm			
	am	pm			
	am	pm			
	am	pm			
	am	pm			
	am	pm			
	am	pm			
	am	pm			

DATE	TIME		SYS/DIA [mmHg]	Heart rate [Pul/min]	NOTES
	am	pm			
	am	pm			
	am	pm			
	am	pm			
	am	pm			
	am	pm			
	am	pm			
	am	pm			
	am	pm			
	am	pm			
	am	pm			
	am	pm			
	am	pm			
	am	pm			
	am	pm			
	am	pm			
	am	pm			

DATE	TIME		SYS/DIA [mmHg]	Heart rate [Pul/min]	NOTES
	am	pm			
	am	pm			
	am	pm			
	am	pm			
	am	pm			
	am	pm			
	am	pm			
	am	pm			
	am	pm			
	am	pm			
	am	pm			
	am	pm			
	am	pm			
	am	pm			
	am	pm			
	am	pm			

DATE	TIME		SYS/DIA [mmHg]	Heart rate [Pul/min]	NOTES
	am	pm			
	am	pm			
	am	pm			
	am	pm			
	am	pm			
	am	pm			
	am	pm			
	am	pm			
	am	pm			
	am	pm			
	am	pm			
	am	pm			
	am	pm			
	am	pm			
	am	pm			
	am	pm			
	am	pm			

DATE	TIME		SYS/DIA [mmHg]	Heart rate [Pul/min]	NOTES
	am	pm			
	am	pm			
	am	pm			
	am	pm			
	am	pm			
	am	pm			
	am	pm			
	am	pm			
	am	pm			
	am	pm			
	am	pm			
	am	pm			
	am	pm			
	am	pm			
	am	pm			
	am	pm			

DATE	TIME		SYS/DIA [mmHg]	Heart rate [Pul/min]	NOTES
	am	pm			
	am	pm			
	am	pm			
	am	pm			
	am	pm			
	am	pm			
	am	pm			
	am	pm			
	am	pm			
	am	pm			
	am	pm			
	am	pm			
	am	pm			
	am	pm			
	am	pm			
	am	pm			
	am	pm			

DATE	TIME		SYS/DIA [mmHg]	Heart rate [Pul/min]	NOTES
	am	pm			
	am	pm			
	am	pm			
	am	pm			
	am	pm			
	am	pm			
	am	pm			
	am	pm			
	am	pm			
	am	pm			
	am	pm			
	am	pm			
	am	pm			
	am	pm			
	am	pm			
	am	pm			

DATE	TIME		SYS/DIA [mmHg]	Heart rate [Pul/min]	NOTES
	am	pm			
	am	pm			
	am	pm			
	am	pm			
	am	pm			
	am	pm			
	am	pm			
	am	pm			
	am	pm			
	am	pm			
	am	pm			
	am	pm			
	am	pm			
	am	pm			
	am	pm			
	am	pm			
	am	pm			

DATE	TIME		SYS/DIA [mmHg]	Heart rate [Pul/min]	NOTES
	am	pm			
	am	pm			
	am	pm			
	am	pm			
	am	pm			
	am	pm			
	am	pm			
	am	pm			
	am	pm			
	am	pm			
	am	pm			
	am	pm			
	am	pm			
	am	pm			
	am	pm			
	am	pm			

DATE	TIME		SYS/DIA [mmHg]	Heart rate [Pul/min]	NOTES
	am	pm			
	am	pm			
	am	pm			
	am	pm			
	am	pm			
	am	pm			
	am	pm			
	am	pm			
	am	pm			
	am	pm			
	am	pm			
	am	pm			
	am	pm			
	am	pm			
	am	pm			
	am	pm			

DATE	TIME		SYS/DIA [mmHg]	Heart rate [Pul/min]	NOTES
	am	pm			
	am	pm			
	am	pm			
	am	pm			
	am	pm			
	am	pm			
	am	pm			
	am	pm			
	am	pm			
	am	pm			
	am	pm			
	am	pm			
	am	pm			
	am	pm			
	am	pm			
	am	pm			

DATE	TIME		SYS/DIA [mmHg]	Heart rate [Pul/min]	NOTES
	am	pm			
	am	pm			
	am	pm			
	am	pm			
	am	pm			
	am	pm			
	am	pm			
	am	pm			
	am	pm			
	am	pm			
	am	pm			
	am	pm			
	am	pm			
	am	pm			
	am	pm			
	am	pm			

DATE	TIME		SYS/DIA [mmHg]	Heart rate [Pul/min]	NOTES
	am	pm			
	am	pm			
	am	pm			
	am	pm			
	am	pm			
	am	pm			
	am	pm			
	am	pm			
	am	pm			
	am	pm			
	am	pm			
	am	pm			
	am	pm			
	am	pm			
	am	pm			
	am	pm			

DATE	TIME		SYS/DIA [mmHg]	Heart rate [Pul/min]	NOTES
	am	pm			
	am	pm			
	am	pm			
	am	pm			
	am	pm			
	am	pm			
	am	pm			
	am	pm			
	am	pm			
	am	pm			
	am	pm			
	am	pm			
	am	pm			
	am	pm			
	am	pm			
	am	pm			
	am	pm			
	am	pm			

DATE	TIME		SYS/DIA [mmHg]	Heart rate [Pul/min]	NOTES
	am	pm			
	am	pm			
	am	pm			
	am	pm			
	am	pm			
	am	pm			
	am	pm			
	am	pm			
	am	pm			
	am	pm			
	am	pm			
	am	pm			
	am	pm			
	am	pm			
	am	pm			
	am	pm			

DATE	TIME		SYS/DIA [mmHg]	Heart rate [Pul/min]	NOTES
	am	pm			
	am	pm			
	am	pm			
	am	pm			
	am	pm			
	am	pm			
	am	pm			
	am	pm			
	am	pm			
	am	pm			
	am	pm			
	am	pm			
	am	pm			
	am	pm			
	am	pm			
	am	pm			

DATE	TIME		SYS/DIA [mmHg]	Heart rate [Pul/min]	NOTES
	am	pm			
	am	pm			
	am	pm			
	am	pm			
	am	pm			
	am	pm			
	am	pm			
	am	pm			
	am	pm			
	am	pm			
	am	pm			
	am	pm			
	am	pm			
	am	pm			
	am	pm			
	am	pm			

DATE	TIME		SYS/DIA [mmHg]	Heart rate [Pul/min]	NOTES
	am	pm			
	am	pm			
	am	pm			
	am	pm			
	am	pm			
	am	pm			
	am	pm			
	am	pm			
	am	pm			
	am	pm			
	am	pm			
	am	pm			
	am	pm			
	am	pm			
	am	pm			
	am	pm			

DATE	TIME		SYS/DIA [mmHg]	Heart rate [Pul/min]	NOTES
	am	pm			
	am	pm			
	am	pm			
	am	pm			
	am	pm			
	am	pm			
	am	pm			
	am	pm			
	am	pm			
	am	pm			
	am	pm			
	am	pm			
	am	pm			
	am	pm			
	am	pm			
	am	pm			

DATE	TIME		SYS/DIA [mmHg]	Heart rate [Pul/min]	NOTES
	am	pm			
	am	pm			
	am	pm			
	am	pm			
	am	pm			
	am	pm			
	am	pm			
	am	pm			
	am	pm			
	am	pm			
	am	pm			
	am	pm			
	am	pm			
	am	pm			
	am	pm			
	am	pm			
	am	pm			
	am	pm			

DATE	TIME		SYS/DIA [mmHg]	Heart rate [Pul/min]	NOTES
	am	pm			
	am	pm			
	am	pm			
	am	pm			
	am	pm			
	am	pm			
	am	pm			
	am	pm			
	am	pm			
	am	pm			
	am	pm			
	am	pm			
	am	pm			
	am	pm			
	am	pm			
	am	pm			

DATE	TIME am	TIME pm	SYS/DIA [mmHg]	Heart rate [Pul/min]	NOTES
	am	pm			
	am	pm			
	am	pm			
	am	pm			
	am	pm			
	am	pm			
	am	pm			
	am	pm			
	am	pm			
	am	pm			
	am	pm			
	am	pm			
	am	pm			
	am	pm			
	am	pm			

DATE	TIME		SYS/DIA [mmHg]	Heart rate [Pul/min]	NOTES
	am	pm			
	am	pm			
	am	pm			
	am	pm			
	am	pm			
	am	pm			
	am	pm			
	am	pm			
	am	pm			
	am	pm			
	am	pm			
	am	pm			
	am	pm			
	am	pm			
	am	pm			
	am	pm			

DATE	TIME		SYS/DIA [mmHg]	Heart rate [Pul/min]	NOTES
	am	pm			
	am	pm			
	am	pm			
	am	pm			
	am	pm			
	am	pm			
	am	pm			
	am	pm			
	am	pm			
	am	pm			
	am	pm			
	am	pm			
	am	pm			
	am	pm			
	am	pm			
	am	pm			
	am	pm			

DATE	TIME		SYS/DIA [mmHg]	Heart rate [Pul/min]	NOTES
	am	pm			
	am	pm			
	am	pm			
	am	pm			
	am	pm			
	am	pm			
	am	pm			
	am	pm			
	am	pm			
	am	pm			
	am	pm			
	am	pm			
	am	pm			
	am	pm			
	am	pm			
	am	pm			

DATE	TIME		SYS/DIA [mmHg]	Heart rate [Pul/min]	NOTES
	am	pm			
	am	pm			
	am	pm			
	am	pm			
	am	pm			
	am	pm			
	am	pm			
	am	pm			
	am	pm			
	am	pm			
	am	pm			
	am	pm			
	am	pm			
	am	pm			
	am	pm			
	am	pm			
	am	pm			
	am	pm			

DATE	TIME		SYS/DIA [mmHg]	Heart rate [Pul/min]	NOTES
	am	pm			
	am	pm			
	am	pm			
	am	pm			
	am	pm			
	am	pm			
	am	pm			
	am	pm			
	am	pm			
	am	pm			
	am	pm			
	am	pm			
	am	pm			
	am	pm			
	am	pm			
	am	pm			

DATE	TIME		SYS/DIA [mmHg]	Heart rate [Pul/min]	NOTES
	am	pm			
	am	pm			
	am	pm			
	am	pm			
	am	pm			
	am	pm			
	am	pm			
	am	pm			
	am	pm			
	am	pm			
	am	pm			
	am	pm			
	am	pm			
	am	pm			
	am	pm			

DATE	TIME		SYS/DIA [mmHg]	Heart rate [Pul/min]	NOTES
	am	pm			
	am	pm			
	am	pm			
	am	pm			
	am	pm			
	am	pm			
	am	pm			
	am	pm			
	am	pm			
	am	pm			
	am	pm			
	am	pm			
	am	pm			
	am	pm			
	am	pm			
	am	pm			

DATE	TIME		SYS/DIA [mmHg]	Heart rate [Pul/min]	NOTES
	am	pm			
	am	pm			
	am	pm			
	am	pm			
	am	pm			
	am	pm			
	am	pm			
	am	pm			
	am	pm			
	am	pm			
	am	pm			
	am	pm			
	am	pm			
	am	pm			
	am	pm			
	am	pm			

DATE	TIME		SYS/DIA [mmHg]	Heart rate [Pul/min]	NOTES
	am	pm			
	am	pm			
	am	pm			
	am	pm			
	am	pm			
	am	pm			
	am	pm			
	am	pm			
	am	pm			
	am	pm			
	am	pm			
	am	pm			
	am	pm			
	am	pm			
	am	pm			
	am	pm			

DATE	TIME		SYS/DIA [mmHg]	Heart rate [Pul/min]	NOTES
	am	pm			
	am	pm			
	am	pm			
	am	pm			
	am	pm			
	am	pm			
	am	pm			
	am	pm			
	am	pm			
	am	pm			
	am	pm			
	am	pm			
	am	pm			
	am	pm			
	am	pm			
	am	pm			
	am	pm			
	am	pm			

DATE	TIME		SYS/DIA [mmHg]	Heart rate [Pul/min]	NOTES
	am	pm			
	am	pm			
	am	pm			
	am	pm			
	am	pm			
	am	pm			
	am	pm			
	am	pm			
	am	pm			
	am	pm			
	am	pm			
	am	pm			
	am	pm			
	am	pm			
	am	pm			
	am	pm			

DATE	TIME		SYS/DIA [mmHg]	Heart rate [Pul/min]	NOTES
	am	pm			
	am	pm			
	am	pm			
	am	pm			
	am	pm			
	am	pm			
	am	pm			
	am	pm			
	am	pm			
	am	pm			
	am	pm			
	am	pm			
	am	pm			
	am	pm			
	am	pm			
	am	pm			
	am	pm			

DATE	TIME		SYS/DIA [mmHg]	Heart rate [Pul/min]	NOTES
	am	pm			
	am	pm			
	am	pm			
	am	pm			
	am	pm			
	am	pm			
	am	pm			
	am	pm			
	am	pm			
	am	pm			
	am	pm			
	am	pm			
	am	pm			
	am	pm			
	am	pm			
	am	pm			

DATE	TIME		SYS/DIA [mmHg]	Heart rate [Pul/min]	NOTES
	am	pm			
	am	pm			
	am	pm			
	am	pm			
	am	pm			
	am	pm			
	am	pm			
	am	pm			
	am	pm			
	am	pm			
	am	pm			
	am	pm			
	am	pm			
	am	pm			
	am	pm			
	am	pm			

DATE	TIME		SYS/DIA [mmHg]	Heart rate [Pul/min]	NOTES
	am	pm			
	am	pm			
	am	pm			
	am	pm			
	am	pm			
	am	pm			
	am	pm			
	am	pm			
	am	pm			
	am	pm			
	am	pm			
	am	pm			
	am	pm			
	am	pm			
	am	pm			
	am	pm			

DATE	TIME		SYS/DIA [mmHg]	Heart rate [Pul/min]	NOTES
	am	pm			
	am	pm			
	am	pm			
	am	pm			
	am	pm			
	am	pm			
	am	pm			
	am	pm			
	am	pm			
	am	pm			
	am	pm			
	am	pm			
	am	pm			
	am	pm			
	am	pm			
	am	pm			
	am	pm			
	am	pm			

DATE	TIME		SYS/DIA [mmHg]	Heart rate [Pul/min]	NOTES
	am	pm			
	am	pm			
	am	pm			
	am	pm			
	am	pm			
	am	pm			
	am	pm			
	am	pm			
	am	pm			
	am	pm			
	am	pm			
	am	pm			
	am	pm			
	am	pm			
	am	pm			
	am	pm			

DATE	TIME		SYS/DIA [mmHg]	Heart rate [Pul/min]	NOTES
	am	pm			
	am	pm			
	am	pm			
	am	pm			
	am	pm			
	am	pm			
	am	pm			
	am	pm			
	am	pm			
	am	pm			
	am	pm			
	am	pm			
	am	pm			
	am	pm			
	am	pm			
	am	pm			
	am	pm			

DATE	TIME		SYS/DIA [mmHg]	Heart rate [Pul/min]	NOTES
	am	pm			
	am	pm			
	am	pm			
	am	pm			
	am	pm			
	am	pm			
	am	pm			
	am	pm			
	am	pm			
	am	pm			
	am	pm			
	am	pm			
	am	pm			
	am	pm			
	am	pm			
	am	pm			

DATE	TIME		SYS/DIA [mmHg]	Heart rate [Pul/min]	NOTES
	am	pm			
	am	pm			
	am	pm			
	am	pm			
	am	pm			
	am	pm			
	am	pm			
	am	pm			
	am	pm			
	am	pm			
	am	pm			
	am	pm			
	am	pm			
	am	pm			
	am	pm			
	am	pm			
	am	pm			

DATE	TIME		SYS/DIA [mmHg]	Heart rate [Pul/min]	NOTES
	am	pm			
	am	pm			
	am	pm			
	am	pm			
	am	pm			
	am	pm			
	am	pm			
	am	pm			
	am	pm			
	am	pm			
	am	pm			
	am	pm			
	am	pm			
	am	pm			
	am	pm			
	am	pm			

DATE	TIME		SYS/DIA [mmHg]	Heart rate [Pul/min]	NOTES
	am	pm			
	am	pm			
	am	pm			
	am	pm			
	am	pm			
	am	pm			
	am	pm			
	am	pm			
	am	pm			
	am	pm			
	am	pm			
	am	pm			
	am	pm			
	am	pm			
	am	pm			
	am	pm			
	am	pm			

DATE	TIME		SYS/DIA [mmHg]	Heart rate [Pul/min]	NOTES
	am	pm			
	am	pm			
	am	pm			
	am	pm			
	am	pm			
	am	pm			
	am	pm			
	am	pm			
	am	pm			
	am	pm			
	am	pm			
	am	pm			
	am	pm			
	am	pm			
	am	pm			
	am	pm			

DATE	TIME		SYS/DIA [mmHg]	Heart rate [Pul/min]	NOTES
	am	pm			
	am	pm			
	am	pm			
	am	pm			
	am	pm			
	am	pm			
	am	pm			
	am	pm			
	am	pm			
	am	pm			
	am	pm			
	am	pm			
	am	pm			
	am	pm			
	am	pm			
	am	pm			
	am	pm			

DATE	TIME		SYS/DIA [mmHg]	Heart rate [Pul/min]	NOTES
	am	pm			
	am	pm			
	am	pm			
	am	pm			
	am	pm			
	am	pm			
	am	pm			
	am	pm			
	am	pm			
	am	pm			
	am	pm			
	am	pm			
	am	pm			
	am	pm			
	am	pm			
	am	pm			

DATE	TIME		SYS/DIA [mmHg]	Heart rate [Pul/min]	NOTES
	am	pm			
	am	pm			
	am	pm			
	am	pm			
	am	pm			
	am	pm			
	am	pm			
	am	pm			
	am	pm			
	am	pm			
	am	pm			
	am	pm			
	am	pm			
	am	pm			
	am	pm			
	am	pm			

DATE	TIME		SYS/DIA [mmHg]	Heart rate [Pul/min]	NOTES
	am	pm			
	am	pm			
	am	pm			
	am	pm			
	am	pm			
	am	pm			
	am	pm			
	am	pm			
	am	pm			
	am	pm			
	am	pm			
	am	pm			
	am	pm			
	am	pm			
	am	pm			
	am	pm			

DATE	TIME		SYS/DIA [mmHg]	Heart rate [Pul/min]	NOTES
	am	pm			
	am	pm			
	am	pm			
	am	pm			
	am	pm			
	am	pm			
	am	pm			
	am	pm			
	am	pm			
	am	pm			
	am	pm			
	am	pm			
	am	pm			
	am	pm			
	am	pm			
	am	pm			
	am	pm			

DATE	TIME		SYS/DIA [mmHg]	Heart rate [Pul/min]	NOTES
	am	pm			
	am	pm			
	am	pm			
	am	pm			
	am	pm			
	am	pm			
	am	pm			
	am	pm			
	am	pm			
	am	pm			
	am	pm			
	am	pm			
	am	pm			
	am	pm			
	am	pm			
	am	pm			

DATE	TIME		SYS/DIA [mmHg]	Heart rate [Pul/min]	NOTES
	am	pm			
	am	pm			
	am	pm			
	am	pm			
	am	pm			
	am	pm			
	am	pm			
	am	pm			
	am	pm			
	am	pm			
	am	pm			
	am	pm			
	am	pm			
	am	pm			
	am	pm			
	am	pm			
	am	pm			

DATE	TIME		SYS/DIA [mmHg]	Heart rate [Pul/min]	NOTES
	am	pm			
	am	pm			
	am	pm			
	am	pm			
	am	pm			
	am	pm			
	am	pm			
	am	pm			
	am	pm			
	am	pm			
	am	pm			
	am	pm			
	am	pm			
	am	pm			
	am	pm			
	am	pm			

DATE	TIME		SYS/DIA [mmHg]	Heart rate [Pul/min]	NOTES
	am	pm			
	am	pm			
	am	pm			
	am	pm			
	am	pm			
	am	pm			
	am	pm			
	am	pm			
	am	pm			
	am	pm			
	am	pm			
	am	pm			
	am	pm			
	am	pm			
	am	pm			
	am	pm			
	am	pm			
	am	pm			

DATE	TIME		SYS/DIA [mmHg]	Heart rate [Pul/min]	NOTES
	am	pm			
	am	pm			
	am	pm			
	am	pm			
	am	pm			
	am	pm			
	am	pm			
	am	pm			
	am	pm			
	am	pm			
	am	pm			
	am	pm			
	am	pm			
	am	pm			
	am	pm			
	am	pm			

DATE	TIME		SYS/DIA [mmHg]	Heart rate [Pul/min]	NOTES
	am	pm			
	am	pm			
	am	pm			
	am	pm			
	am	pm			
	am	pm			
	am	pm			
	am	pm			
	am	pm			
	am	pm			
	am	pm			
	am	pm			
	am	pm			
	am	pm			
	am	pm			
	am	pm			

DATE	TIME		SYS/DIA [mmHg]	Heart rate [Pul/min]	NOTES
	am	pm			
	am	pm			
	am	pm			
	am	pm			
	am	pm			
	am	pm			
	am	pm			
	am	pm			
	am	pm			
	am	pm			
	am	pm			
	am	pm			
	am	pm			
	am	pm			
	am	pm			

DATE	TIME		SYS/DIA [mmHg]	Heart rate [Pul/min]	NOTES
	am	pm			
	am	pm			
	am	pm			
	am	pm			
	am	pm			
	am	pm			
	am	pm			
	am	pm			
	am	pm			
	am	pm			
	am	pm			
	am	pm			
	am	pm			
	am	pm			
	am	pm			
	am	pm			
	am	pm			

DATE	TIME		SYS/DIA [mmHg]	Heart rate [Pul/min]	NOTES
	am	pm			
	am	pm			
	am	pm			
	am	pm			
	am	pm			
	am	pm			
	am	pm			
	am	pm			
	am	pm			
	am	pm			
	am	pm			
	am	pm			
	am	pm			
	am	pm			
	am	pm			

DATE	TIME		SYS/DIA [mmHg]	Heart rate [Pul/min]	NOTES
	am	pm			
	am	pm			
	am	pm			
	am	pm			
	am	pm			
	am	pm			
	am	pm			
	am	pm			
	am	pm			
	am	pm			
	am	pm			
	am	pm			
	am	pm			
	am	pm			
	am	pm			
	am	pm			
	am	pm			

DATE	TIME		SYS/DIA [mmHg]	Heart rate [Pul/min]	NOTES
	am	pm			
	am	pm			
	am	pm			
	am	pm			
	am	pm			
	am	pm			
	am	pm			
	am	pm			
	am	pm			
	am	pm			
	am	pm			
	am	pm			
	am	pm			
	am	pm			
	am	pm			
	am	pm			

DATE	TIME		SYS/DIA [mmHg]	Heart rate [Pul/min]	NOTES
	am	pm			
	am	pm			
	am	pm			
	am	pm			
	am	pm			
	am	pm			
	am	pm			
	am	pm			
	am	pm			
	am	pm			
	am	pm			
	am	pm			
	am	pm			
	am	pm			
	am	pm			
	am	pm			

DATE	TIME		SYS/DIA [mmHg]	Heart rate [Pul/min]	NOTES
	am	pm			
	am	pm			
	am	pm			
	am	pm			
	am	pm			
	am	pm			
	am	pm			
	am	pm			
	am	pm			
	am	pm			
	am	pm			
	am	pm			
	am	pm			
	am	pm			
	am	pm			
	am	pm			

DATE	TIME		SYS/DIA [mmHg]	Heart rate [Pul/min]	NOTES
	am	pm			
	am	pm			
	am	pm			
	am	pm			
	am	pm			
	am	pm			
	am	pm			
	am	pm			
	am	pm			
	am	pm			
	am	pm			
	am	pm			
	am	pm			
	am	pm			
	am	pm			
	am	pm			
	am	pm			

DATE	TIME		SYS/DIA [mmHg]	Heart rate [Pul/min]	NOTES
	am	pm			
	am	pm			
	am	pm			
	am	pm			
	am	pm			
	am	pm			
	am	pm			
	am	pm			
	am	pm			
	am	pm			
	am	pm			
	am	pm			
	am	pm			
	am	pm			
	am	pm			
	am	pm			

DATE	TIME		SYS/DIA [mmHg]	Heart rate [Pul/min]	NOTES
	am	pm			
	am	pm			
	am	pm			
	am	pm			
	am	pm			
	am	pm			
	am	pm			
	am	pm			
	am	pm			
	am	pm			
	am	pm			
	am	pm			
	am	pm			
	am	pm			
	am	pm			
	am	pm			

DATE	TIME		SYS/DIA [mmHg]	Heart rate [Pul/min]	NOTES
	am	pm			
	am	pm			
	am	pm			
	am	pm			
	am	pm			
	am	pm			
	am	pm			
	am	pm			
	am	pm			
	am	pm			
	am	pm			
	am	pm			
	am	pm			
	am	pm			
	am	pm			
	am	pm			

DATE	TIME		SYS/DIA [mmHg]	Heart rate [Pul/min]	NOTES
	am	pm			
	am	pm			
	am	pm			
	am	pm			
	am	pm			
	am	pm			
	am	pm			
	am	pm			
	am	pm			
	am	pm			
	am	pm			
	am	pm			
	am	pm			
	am	pm			
	am	pm			
	am	pm			
	am	pm			

DATE	TIME		SYS/DIA [mmHg]	Heart rate [Pul/min]	NOTES
	am	pm			
	am	pm			
	am	pm			
	am	pm			
	am	pm			
	am	pm			
	am	pm			
	am	pm			
	am	pm			
	am	pm			
	am	pm			
	am	pm			
	am	pm			
	am	pm			
	am	pm			
	am	pm			
	am	pm			

DATE	TIME		SYS/DIA [mmHg]	Heart rate [Pul/min]	NOTES
	am	pm			
	am	pm			
	am	pm			
	am	pm			
	am	pm			
	am	pm			
	am	pm			
	am	pm			
	am	pm			
	am	pm			
	am	pm			
	am	pm			
	am	pm			
	am	pm			
	am	pm			
	am	pm			

DATE	TIME		SYS/DIA [mmHg]	Heart rate [Pul/min]	NOTES
	am	pm			
	am	pm			
	am	pm			
	am	pm			
	am	pm			
	am	pm			
	am	pm			
	am	pm			
	am	pm			
	am	pm			
	am	pm			
	am	pm			
	am	pm			
	am	pm			
	am	pm			

DATE	TIME		SYS/DIA [mmHg]	Heart rate [Pul/min]	NOTES
	am	pm			
	am	pm			
	am	pm			
	am	pm			
	am	pm			
	am	pm			
	am	pm			
	am	pm			
	am	pm			
	am	pm			
	am	pm			
	am	pm			
	am	pm			
	am	pm			
	am	pm			
	am	pm			

DATE	TIME		SYS/DIA [mmHg]	Heart rate [Pul/min]	NOTES
	am	pm			
	am	pm			
	am	pm			
	am	pm			
	am	pm			
	am	pm			
	am	pm			
	am	pm			
	am	pm			
	am	pm			
	am	pm			
	am	pm			
	am	pm			
	am	pm			
	am	pm			
	am	pm			

DATE	TIME		SYS/DIA [mmHg]	Heart rate [Pul/min]	NOTES
	am	pm			
	am	pm			
	am	pm			
	am	pm			
	am	pm			
	am	pm			
	am	pm			
	am	pm			
	am	pm			
	am	pm			
	am	pm			
	am	pm			
	am	pm			
	am	pm			
	am	pm			
	am	pm			
	am	pm			

DATE	TIME		SYS/DIA [mmHg]	Heart rate [Pul/min]	NOTES
	am	pm			
	am	pm			
	am	pm			
	am	pm			
	am	pm			
	am	pm			
	am	pm			
	am	pm			
	am	pm			
	am	pm			
	am	pm			
	am	pm			
	am	pm			
	am	pm			
	am	pm			
	am	pm			

DATE	TIME		SYS/DIA [mmHg]	Heart rate [Pul/min]	NOTES
	am	pm			
	am	pm			
	am	pm			
	am	pm			
	am	pm			
	am	pm			
	am	pm			
	am	pm			
	am	pm			
	am	pm			
	am	pm			
	am	pm			
	am	pm			
	am	pm			
	am	pm			
	am	pm			
	am	pm			

DATE	TIME		SYS/DIA [mmHg]	Heart rate [Pul/min]	NOTES
	am	pm			
	am	pm			
	am	pm			
	am	pm			
	am	pm			
	am	pm			
	am	pm			
	am	pm			
	am	pm			
	am	pm			
	am	pm			
	am	pm			
	am	pm			
	am	pm			
	am	pm			

DATE	TIME		SYS/DIA [mmHg]	Heart rate [Pul/min]	NOTES
	am	pm			
	am	pm			
	am	pm			
	am	pm			
	am	pm			
	am	pm			
	am	pm			
	am	pm			
	am	pm			
	am	pm			
	am	pm			
	am	pm			
	am	pm			
	am	pm			
	am	pm			
	am	pm			
	am	pm			

DATE	TIME		SYS/DIA [mmHg]	Heart rate [Pul/min]	NOTES
	am	pm			
	am	pm			
	am	pm			
	am	pm			
	am	pm			
	am	pm			
	am	pm			
	am	pm			
	am	pm			
	am	pm			
	am	pm			
	am	pm			
	am	pm			
	am	pm			
	am	pm			
	am	pm			

DATE	TIME		SYS/DIA [mmHg]	Heart rate [Pul/min]	NOTES
	am	pm			
	am	pm			
	am	pm			
	am	pm			
	am	pm			
	am	pm			
	am	pm			
	am	pm			
	am	pm			
	am	pm			
	am	pm			
	am	pm			
	am	pm			
	am	pm			
	am	pm			
	am	pm			
	am	pm			

DATE	TIME		SYS/DIA [mmHg]	Heart rate [Pul/min]	NOTES
	am	pm			
	am	pm			
	am	pm			
	am	pm			
	am	pm			
	am	pm			
	am	pm			
	am	pm			
	am	pm			
	am	pm			
	am	pm			
	am	pm			
	am	pm			
	am	pm			
	am	pm			

DATE	TIME		SYS/DIA [mmHg]	Heart rate [Pul/min]	NOTES
	am	pm			
	am	pm			
	am	pm			
	am	pm			
	am	pm			
	am	pm			
	am	pm			
	am	pm			
	am	pm			
	am	pm			
	am	pm			
	am	pm			
	am	pm			
	am	pm			
	am	pm			
	am	pm			

DATE	TIME		SYS/DIA [mmHg]	Heart rate [Pul/min]	NOTES
	am	pm			
	am	pm			
	am	pm			
	am	pm			
	am	pm			
	am	pm			
	am	pm			
	am	pm			
	am	pm			
	am	pm			
	am	pm			
	am	pm			
	am	pm			
	am	pm			
	am	pm			
	am	pm			

DATE	TIME		SYS/DIA [mmHg]	Heart rate [Pul/min]	NOTES
	am	pm			
	am	pm			
	am	pm			
	am	pm			
	am	pm			
	am	pm			
	am	pm			
	am	pm			
	am	pm			
	am	pm			
	am	pm			
	am	pm			
	am	pm			
	am	pm			
	am	pm			
	am	pm			

DATE	TIME		SYS/DIA [mmHg]	Heart rate [Pul/min]	NOTES
	am	pm			
	am	pm			
	am	pm			
	am	pm			
	am	pm			
	am	pm			
	am	pm			
	am	pm			
	am	pm			
	am	pm			
	am	pm			
	am	pm			
	am	pm			
	am	pm			
	am	pm			
	am	pm			

DATE	TIME		SYS/DIA [mmHg]	Heart rate [Pul/min]	NOTES
	am	pm			
	am	pm			
	am	pm			
	am	pm			
	am	pm			
	am	pm			
	am	pm			
	am	pm			
	am	pm			
	am	pm			
	am	pm			
	am	pm			
	am	pm			
	am	pm			
	am	pm			
	am	pm			

DATE	TIME		SYS/DIA [mmHg]	Heart rate [Pul/min]	NOTES
	am	pm			
	am	pm			
	am	pm			
	am	pm			
	am	pm			
	am	pm			
	am	pm			
	am	pm			
	am	pm			
	am	pm			
	am	pm			
	am	pm			
	am	pm			
	am	pm			
	am	pm			
	am	pm			

DATE	TIME		SYS/DIA [mmHg]	Heart rate [Pul/min]	NOTES
	am	pm			
	am	pm			
	am	pm			
	am	pm			
	am	pm			
	am	pm			
	am	pm			
	am	pm			
	am	pm			
	am	pm			
	am	pm			
	am	pm			
	am	pm			
	am	pm			
	am	pm			
	am	pm			

DATE	TIME		SYS/DIA [mmHg]	Heart rate [Pul/min]	NOTES
	am	pm			
	am	pm			
	am	pm			
	am	pm			
	am	pm			
	am	pm			
	am	pm			
	am	pm			
	am	pm			
	am	pm			
	am	pm			
	am	pm			
	am	pm			
	am	pm			
	am	pm			
	am	pm			

DATE	TIME		SYS/DIA [mmHg]	Heart rate [Pul/min]	NOTES
	am	pm			
	am	pm			
	am	pm			
	am	pm			
	am	pm			
	am	pm			
	am	pm			
	am	pm			
	am	pm			
	am	pm			
	am	pm			
	am	pm			
	am	pm			
	am	pm			
	am	pm			
	am	pm			

DATE	TIME		SYS/DIA [mmHg]	Heart rate [Pul/min]	NOTES
	am	pm			
	am	pm			
	am	pm			
	am	pm			
	am	pm			
	am	pm			
	am	pm			
	am	pm			
	am	pm			
	am	pm			
	am	pm			
	am	pm			
	am	pm			
	am	pm			
	am	pm			
	am	pm			

DATE	TIME		SYS/DIA [mmHg]	Heart rate [Pul/min]	NOTES
	am	pm			
	am	pm			
	am	pm			
	am	pm			
	am	pm			
	am	pm			
	am	pm			
	am	pm			
	am	pm			
	am	pm			
	am	pm			
	am	pm			
	am	pm			
	am	pm			
	am	pm			
	am	pm			
	am	pm			

DATE	TIME		SYS/DIA [mmHg]	Heart rate [Pul/min]	NOTES
	am	pm			
	am	pm			
	am	pm			
	am	pm			
	am	pm			
	am	pm			
	am	pm			
	am	pm			
	am	pm			
	am	pm			
	am	pm			
	am	pm			
	am	pm			
	am	pm			
	am	pm			
	am	pm			

Made in the USA
Las Vegas, NV
15 January 2024

84441255R00057